MW01118156

I WAS A STRANGER

AND YOU TOOK ME IN

MATTHEW 25:35

BY LORAN PERRY

FOREWARD

At the time of the writing of this book we have three adult
adopted children who were snatched from the clutches of
death and the bondage of slavery, given a chance to
experience life and God's love. This writing was not
intended to be a biography of the Perry family. I have
included some of these facts merely to show how God
orchestrated and prepared our lives so that these three
children miraculously given to us by Him, could be
integrated into our family and become so much a part of us
that there was and is absolutely no difference between
them and our natural born children. Their lives have not
necessarily been easy living in a large family with limited
resources. But if you were to ask them I am sure they
would have no regrets, and for sure Carol and I have no
regrets. We mortgaged our lives to pull this thing off and
God has been with us every step of the way. We observed
miracle after miracle as God ran ahead of us. There is no
doubt in my mind that God has great things in mind for
these precious ones that He saved through us as well as for
our other nine children who have witnessed God's
goodness as they walked through these miracles with us.

Loran Perry

CHAPTER ONE

It was a hot sultry afternoon, and the jungle was steaming as the gleaming Boeing 747 touched down at the Airport in San Paulo, Brazil. Carol had been traveling since early morning and she was tired and apprehensive as she walked from the plane into the baggage area. Her mind went back to the last words her husband, Loran had whispered in her ear as they tearfully parted at the terminal in Sioux Falls. "Keep your eyes on the goal. Keep your eyes on the goal. God has sent you on this mission and He will take care of you."

That thought brought a moment of comfort but it quickly

faded as her eyes began to dart around the huge room. People were milling around, looking for their baggage, connecting with friends and causing a general commotion. "They promised to have someone here waiting for me," she muttered under her breath. Her heart leaped in her throat and panic began to seize her as she looked around frantically for a friendly face. It seemed like hundreds of dark brown eyes were all staring at her from under a mop of slick black hair. Over in the corner a young boy with blonde hair stood holding a sign with a name on it but it said "Nancy" so that was of no help. Carol was really starting to panic now, the place was so big and it seemed like all the people were pointing and talking about her in another language. She stood out so differently with her Norwegian fair skin and her golden blonde hair. She began to pray as she fought back the tears.

2

"God, I need you now to help me find the people who were
supposed to meet me." She spied a phone booth over in the
corner and hurried over to it. There was a dark haired
swarthy man using it, so she paced back and forth
nervously in his view, hoping to hurry him up. Finally he
hung up the receiver and stepped out so Carol grabbed the
phone. "Oh no!" she exclaimed out loud, "I don't have
my paper with Nilda's number on it and I only remember
part of it! I'll call Loran he will know what to do!" It was
an old fashioned rotary phone, so she stuck her finger in
the"0" and dialed the operator. A thick drawling voice
came on with words she couldn't understand.

"English, English," she cried frantically, but the same
drawling voice kept asking for her information. Carol hung
up the phone, crying in desperation.

"Why God, Why," she sobbed, "I followed your leading,
I've tried not to run ahead of you." She slumped onto a

3

rough wooden bench alongside the telephone booth. She closed her eyes, trying to shut out the scenes before her that she didn't want to deal with. Her mind went back to autumn two years ago and how it all began.

Loran was sitting in the swing on the patio, gazing up into the evening sky, watching the stars pop out. Carol came out of the house and sat down beside him.

"Can I talk to you for a minute?" she asked.

"Sure," her husband replied, "go ahead."

"I know nine children is a big family and a lot of responsibility, but somehow I don't feel that we are done."

"Yes dear, I think you are truly amazing the way you have suffered through nine very difficult pregnancies, had nine natural deliveries, especially the first one where you had to have one hundred and twenty five stitches to get put back together, most women would have quit there but you loved children too much to give up, and then the last one where

4

the doctor let you go a month overdue and you gave birth to a twelve pounder, but you know what the doctor said," he replied.

"No I'm talking about adoption," was her reply.

"Oh yea, that dream God gave you."

"Please don't make light of it," Carol said, "you know how I have always loved children and wanted to do something special for them."

"Yes I know," Loran said, "I have to admit that you have always had a passion for helping kids and you have always been so good at taking care of them. Looking back over the years I can certainly see God's hand in preparing you for something special, but Nate is still just a baby."

"But we have to start now because we are not getting any younger and the paperwork might take quite a while."

"Well O K, what do you suggest?" Loran asked.

"Next week when we're in Sioux Falls, let's stop at

Lutheran Social Services."

"Great," he replied, glad to be off the hook for the moment.

He knew, however, that they probably would be in Sioux

Falls next week as they were almost every week picking up

supplies for their growing electrical contracting business.

So, all too soon next week came and they found themselves

in Sioux Falls, Loran had finished loading supplies and

began looking for the office of Lutheran Social Services.

As they pulled up in front of the place Loran took a deep

breath and said, "Well let's get started on our new venture."

The lady at the front desk was very cordial. When she

found out that they were interested in adoption, she gave

them an application to fill out and they sat down in the

waiting room and began filling in information on the packet

of papers that the lady had given them. Presently, they

were escorted into an office where an older, grey haired

lady sat behind a large mahogany desk. They gave her

their application. As she began to read, they could see the incredulous look come on her face. "I'm very sorry," she began, "but we have many people on our waiting list who have no children and they have been waiting for years. Why, if you have nine children already, do you need another child?"

"Oh we don't need another child," Carol said, "but it has been a lifelong dream of mine to have a ministry to care for little children."

"Well I certainly appreciate that," the lady said, looking at her over her glasses, "but I'm afraid we won't be able to help you." She thought for a moment, as she shuffled the papers on the huge desk in front of her, and then she said, "Have you ever considered foster care? There is a great need out there for people who truly care."

"I could never do that," replied Carol, "I could never give them up once I took them into my home and learned to love them and care for them."

"Well, there is a magazine here that talks about foreign adoptions," the lady replied, "It's called the OURS magazine, It's the only copy I that have, but I can give you the back page with the address."

"Thank you very much," Carol said, trying not to let her disappointment show. She fought back the tears as they headed out the door.

When they got back in the car and headed home there was "Silence in Heaven for the space of half an hour," she was counting sign posts on her side and he was counting corn rows on his. Carol finally looked at her husband and they both burst out laughing, thinking of the look on the lady's face and how ridiculous they must have looked to her.

"Well at least we can still laugh," said Loran.

"Yes, but we don't have to give up," Carol replied, "We

haven't begun to fight."

Being familiar with her Norwegian heritage and her stubborn nature, Loran knew only too well what she meant. Carol began studying the page of the OURS magazine that the lady had given her.

"There's a phone number here of a couple in Minnesota who had adopted from Brazil, let's call them when we get home."

"Sounds like a good place to start." Loran said.

They arrived home and no sooner got through the door and Carol was on the phone talking to the couple in Minnesota who had adopted from Brazil. Thinking back later, Loran couldn't even remember their name, but they were so excited and they encouraged Carol to push forward with her desire to adopt and that foreign adoption was the way to go.

"Well," said Loran, "as long as God keeps opening doors

we'd better keep walking through them." Looking back at

that point, it was easy to see God's hand leading and

guiding every step of the way.

While talking to the couple, Carol got the name, Carla

Huston, as their contact in Minneapolis. Of course Carol

couldn't wait to talk to her and found out that she was

originally from Lake Preston, a little town just thirty miles

west of Brookings, where the Perrys lived. Mrs. Huston

was so thrilled to find out that someone from her home area

was considering adoption. Carol immediately made an

appointment to meet with her at her home in Minneapolis.

It was later that week when the Perrys arrived at the Huston

home and were greeted by two lovely adopted Korean girls.

They were so cute and sweet they melted Carol's heart

immediately. Carol formed a special bond with Mrs.

Huston also. On one of their later trips to Minneapolis the

Hustons gave the Perrys an igloo shaped jungle gym and

they hauled it home on top of their motor home. Can you imagine seeing a motor home going down the highway with a green and white jungle gym on the roof?

Carla Huston was affiliated with IAAA, International Aid and Adoption Association. They were based in Denver Colorado. They later relocated to Michigan. Loran started making application with them but they informed him that his first hurdle was to get a home study done. They could suggest plenty of qualified people to do it for them in Minnesota, but lo and behold there didn't seem to be anyone certified in South Dakota. Again Carol and Loran were heartsick.

"The enemy is fighting us again," Carol said disgustedly.

"Yes but God is bigger and He didn't bring us this far to leave us sitting," said Loran. "Maybe we should move to Minnesota for a year."

11

"Wouldn't that be hard to do with our business?"

"Yes I would have to commute every day," he said,

"There's got to be another way."

The next day Carol called her cousin, Janet Solberg, they had been close friends since childhood. They had grown up together and were more like sisters than cousins. Carol asked Janet to put her need on the church prayer chain. It wasn't long before the phone rang.

"Carol, this Janet, I heard there is a family North of Volga who adopted, maybe you could ask them how they got their home study done."

"Oh thank you so much!" Carol exclaimed, "Do you have their phone number?"

Carol wrote down the number and quickly dialed the phone. When the lady answered, Carol said, "Hello, you don't know me but my name is Carol Perry, my husband Loran and I live in Brookings and own a business called

Perry Electric, we are trying to adopt and I heard that you folks did and an adoption so I am curious to know how you got your home study done?"

"Well," the lady hesitated a moment, "That did prove to be quite a challenge, but we finally found a man in Brookings by the name of Ted Kemp. He works at the mental health center but he was grandfathered into the certification program when it began so all we had to do was to contact him."

Carol thanked the lady and immediately called the mental health center and made an appointment with Mr. Kemp. When Carol and Loran met with him, they explained that they were not trying to increase their family; but that they felt they were in a ministry to help children and that they had very little money. Unfortunately that went right over his egotistical head because he would bring his family over to the Perry house, line them up on the davenport, tell the

13

Perrys all about HIS troubles, and then send them bill for five hundred dollars! Anyway, he did this a few times and finally completed the home study so Loran could start filling out forms for the immigration service. There were dozens of forms to submit and each one had to be stamped by the Indian Consulate at forty five dollars each. Along with this they found out that they had to have some references from the community. Of course the pastor of their local church was the first one they approached. Sitting in the Pastor's office, they began to tell him of their plans to adopt a foreign child. Loran looked up at Pastor and he was grinning from ear to ear.

"I think it's a great idea," he said, "What can I do to help?"

"We just need a reference, Pastor," said Carol.

"Consider it done," was the Pastor's enthusiastic reply.

So that was easy enough but they had to have at least two

more.

"Well I guess it's time to lean on our business contacts,"
Loran said. Two of the main contractors that he worked for
in town were Harvey Mortinson and Paul Mason. Loran
was in Harvey's office the next morning and found Him
more than willing to be of assistance. Not only that but he
wanted to know if he could contribute to the project. Paul
Mason was next on Loran's agenda and he found him
equally cooperative. Carol and Loran felt so blessed.

"Finally, I think we have everything ready," Loran said.

"Good," Carol replied. "Let's get it sent off to the agency."

"We need to pray over it first," he said ," we need to stay in
step with God every step of the way. You know what
Psalm 37:5 says, Commit your way to the Lord, trust also
in Him, and He shall bring it to pass."

So Loran packaged up the dossier and sent it off to IAAA,

and the tense waiting began.

Every few weeks Carol would call Mrs. Huston to see if there was any news.

"We just have to have patience," she would say.

Of course with Carol's Norwegian background she was anything but patient no matter how hard she tried, and Loran would have to admit with all the work they had put in and all the borrowed money they had invested, he was more than a little bit anxious also. As the weeks turned into months, Carol would call but there was no visible progress. It had been almost a year, and Carol was talking to Nancy at the agency and Nancy said, "I'm very sorry, Mrs. Perry, but the India program is at a standstill, I think you should look elsewhere."

"But I don't know where else to look," Carol replied.

"I do have a phone number of a lady in New York who is working with a couple in Brazil," Nancy said, "I think her

16

name is Alice."

"Alright," said Carol, "I will try to get in contact with her. Thank you for your help."

So Carol contacted Alice and she got all the paperwork in order and put her in contact with Jane and Carl Blomberg who were in Rio De Janero at the time. When Carol talked to them they seemed abrupt and almost rude, and it seemed strange to Carol that they needed a thousand dollars in advance before she could even travel, but being new to this sort of thing she didn't know what to expect. The Perrys didn't have any other options at the time, so Loran just borrowed the money and wired it to them. Soon they contacted Carol again and informed her that they had a set of twins for her, a boy and a girl. Loran hurried and got Carol a passport and an airline ticket. She also had to get a Power of Attorney so she could sign for Loran when she was there. Carol was so worried about losing her passport that her daughters got her a special pouch to put it in and

hung it around her neck. The plan was for her to fly to

New York, meet with Alice, then fly from there to Rio.

The day finally came, January sixth nineteen eighty one,

Carol and Loran were headed for the Sioux Falls airport.

They couldn't help but think back to the day they traveled

that same road coming back from Lutheran Social Services,

how discouraged they were then but they didn't give up.

The words came to Loran, "keep your eye on the goal." He

had been wondering what words of encouragement he

would have for Carol when the time came for her to board

the plane. Here was a country girl who wouldn't go to

Sioux Falls by herself, who was about to leave her two and

one half year old son, four other children still at home, and

her husband, to step off into an adventure that she had no

idea where it would take her. All she knew was that God

had called her to a ministry, and she was doing her best to

be obedient.

The parting at the gate was a tearful one, but she just kept repeating the words that her husband had given her, "Keep your eye on the goal."

The flight to New York was uneventful and Alice was waiting at the gate. She was a very pleasant middle aged lady who was so warm and helpful. They visited while Carol waited for her flight to board. They said their goodbyes and Carol started down the boarding ramp when she started to feel faint. She collapsed against the rail clutching her passport; she was so afraid that someone would take it. A kind gentleman who was going on the same flight came to her rescue and helped her to a place to sit down and got her a cold drink of water.

"My passport, my passport," she kept saying.

When she was feeling better, he helped her on the plane

and to her seat. The trouble was that before she left home, her wedding ring had broken so she couldn't wear it. Her daughter Pam was determined that her mom would not travel out of town with out a ring so she bought her a dime store one to wear. This guy was not to be fooled that easily, however, and he tried to coerce her to go to with him to his city. He was so insistent that the stewardess finally had to move him to another seat. It was a long night on the plane but Carol didn't dare close her eyes, even though the steward and the stewardess kept an eye on him all the time.

When the plane landed in Rio, Carol hurried off the plane and looked frantically around for someone to pick her up. A heavy set, middle aged man approached and said,

"Are you Carol Perry?"

"Yes I am," Carol said, relieved to know she'd been found.

"I'm Carl Blomberg," the man said with a hearty

handshake, "my wife Jane is at home with your babies."

He helped Carol with her bags and put them in the trunk of

his rather beat up old black sedan.

"Get in," he said, "I will show you our home, by the way,

will your husband be able to send me some more money

soon?"

"I'll call him tonight," she said.

As Carol opened the car door she heard a voice within her

say, "these are not your babies." This shook her as she

began to wonder why God had brought her here and what

this ill fated trip was all about. As Carl sped off through

the narrow streets, Carol found herself clinging frantically

to the armrest until her knuckles were white. The car

turned up a steep incline and began winding its way up a

hill. As the car careened into a small driveway, Carol

looked on up the hill and saw the famous statue of Christ

on the hilltop above the city. The house was small and very basic with no yard and very close neighbors. As they entered the house, Jane met Carol and took her to a small bedroom with a crib in the corner. There lay two beautiful little babies with only a rag for a diaper.

"Oh, they are so tiny," Carol exclaimed as she picked the little boy up. She noticed right away that he was feverish and having trouble breathing. "We need to get him to a hospital right away," said Carol.

Jane immediately seemed offended as if she were being accused of not caring for him properly.

"Where is the nearest hospital?" Carol was insistent.

"There is a small clinic about two miles from here," said Carl.

"This baby needs help," Carol was more insistent, "he can barely breathe." She grabbed a tattered old blanket and wrapped the baby in it.

"Please hurry," she cried, "he needs help."

Soon they were back in the car again careening wildly down the steep grade and onto the main thoroughfare, headed for the local clinic. Carol was clutching the baby in her arms and hanging on as best she could.

As they entered the clinic Carol was appalled at what she saw. This was obviously just a clinic for poor people. There were children laying everywhere, some unattended or abandoned. Her heart cried out, "Oh Lord, there are so many needs."

Her first challenge was that she couldn't speak the language. She handed the baby to the nurse and through motions and gestures she was able to get them to work on getting the fever down and getting him some nourishment. Carol stayed at the clinic through the night, hovering over the crib singing and praying over the tiny infant.

As she stood and gazed down at the little bundle, again the

voice inside her came,

"Those are not your babies."

As the next day wore on, Carol was taken back to the house to rest. She went into the bedroom and checked the little girl to see if she was alright. She stroked her tiny head as the tears welled up in her eyes. She had struggled so hard to get here, was she to give up now? She wanted to talk to her husband.

"May I use the phone?" she asked as she came out of the bedroom, "I need to call my husband."

"Sure," said Jane, "remember there is four hours difference in time between here and South Dakota."

Carol took the phone and started dialing, but the next hurdle she faced was finding an operator who could understand English. Finally the phone rang and Loran picked it up. He soon realized it was Carol on the other end and she was telling him all that had happened and asking, "What should I do?" They cried a little together, and then he reminded her to "keep her eye on the goal" She told him how God told her that she needed to learn to trust Him, and this was just a dress rehearsal for what was coming. Loran told her how none of the medical expenses could be covered by their insurance until they were in the United States. Loran could tell that Carol was uneasy about the seemly strange religion that the Blombergs were into, so together they decided it was time for her to come home to regroup and start over. So Carol said to Jane,

"Could I speak to you in the bedroom?"

"What is it?" said Jane, as she entered the room, already suspecting what this was about.

"God has shown me that these are not my babies," said Carol, "I need to return home but I want you to keep us on your list."

"Yes, I suppose we can do that if that's how you feel," said Jane, "but I can't promise you when we will have another baby for you."

"God will provide," Carol replied, "I'm sorry I put you through all this trouble but I have to follow God's leading."

"We will take you to the airport in the morning, good night."

Carol was alone in the room and she lay down and tried to sleep, but her mind was whirling with all that had happened in the last few days. Morning couldn't come soon enough and Carol was so relieved to be back on the plane and headed home. When the plane touched down in New York, she wanted to get down and kiss the ground she was so thankful to be back in the United States. She hurried to the telephone to call home.

"Hi honey, I'm in New York," Loran heard as he picked up

the phone, "I'll be in Sioux Falls at nine thirty tonight."

"We will be there to meet you," he replied, "I bet you are anxious to see the kids."

"Bring them all along, will you please."

"You bet I will," was the reply.

And so it was a tearful and bittersweet reunion as Carol came home empty handed. They had seemingly lost this round but the battle was surely not over.

As winter turned into spring, Carol would check with the agency but there was nothing moving. Then one day Loran picked up the Sioux Falls paper and there was a story about a lady from Sioux Falls who had gone to Brazil to adopt a baby, and while she was there, the couple she was adopting a baby from, was arrested and put in jail for black marketing babies. The lady had her baby, but had no papers and no way to get him out of the country. Then they knew why God had sent Carol home empty handed.

They heard rumors that six months later the poor woman was still there trying to get her baby out of the country. How awful! Carol never heard from the Blombergs again.

One evening Carol and Loran were surprised by a visit from their son Keven and his wife Deb. She looked rather long faced and somber as they sat down on the davenport. Carol sensing there was something wrong, said, "Deb what's the matter." The tears began to flow as she began to express her concerns. "We heard you are trying to adopt and we will be starting our family soon and I'm afraid that if you have your own little one you won't be able to be a grandma and grandpa to our babies!"

Carol and Loran both jumped to Deb's side and began to hug her.

"Oh Deb please don't worry about that," exclaimed Carol, "you know our hearts; you know we have love enough to go around. You just bring us those babies and we will love them as much as any grandparents could." Deb smiled through her tears gave them both a big hug. What a blessing to have such a concerned and loving family.

Then came the day in late May when Carol got frustrated and tired of waiting and said, "There must be someone who can help us. Where can we find someone from another country who can make connections for us?"

"There are people from other countries at the university," Loran responded.

"I'm going to call there right now."

"Here's the number for the foreign language department," he said.

In a few minutes, Carol came back excited.

"They let me talk to a young man named Ramoen from Brazil. He gave me the name of a pastor, Carlos Demos, who is a Brazilian, that helped him to get here, and he lives in Harrisburg South Dakota. Will you help me find his number?"

"I'll call information, it shouldn't be too hard to find."

So Carol called this pastor and set up an appointment with him the following afternoon. Harrisburg is just a few miles south of Sioux Falls so it only took a little over an hour to get there. It is a small town and they had no trouble finding his address. As he greeted them at the door, Carol said, "we need to pray," so they immediately sat down at the table and prayed together that God would bless this venture and that His will would be done in every step of the way. Pastor Demos told them how he had helped Ramoen to get a passport and raise the funds to get to Brookings and get enrolled at South Dakota State University. Then he told how he knew a missionary couple who lived in California that had a friend whose name was Nilda, living in Londrina Brazil. Can you believe that lady ran a home for unwed mothers? He didn't know how much English the lady spoke, so he said, "Let's call her from here right now." After talking to her for a while he found out that she did speak some broken English, but the awesome thing he discovered was that even though most all of the women that came to her home kept their babies, just the night before a young girl had come to her place with her sad story. She was blonde, blue eyed, of German decent, but illiterate, her only job was cleaning houses and she had a blind grandmother to take care of. She said there was no way she could take care of her little brown skinned baby. So she left her with Nilda, signed off on her with a thumb print, and disappeared into the night. Nilda knew if the baby had stayed with her mother she would have become someone's house slave because that is what usually happened in situations like this. So she was just beginning to try to figure out what to do with the seven pound, five ounce baby girl with lots of dark hair. Pastor Demos explained that he had a couple at his house that was interested in adopting the child. Carol was so excited that she could hardly speak. She could hear God in her spirit saying, "If you hadn't have been patient you would have missed Kalee." Nilda needed a name for the baby right away so Carol gave her the name Kalee but Nilda got it mixed up and put Kelly on the papers so they had to deal with that later too. Carol's passport was still valid so in a matter of a few days she went from frustrated to flying. With stops in St. Louis, Miami, and Rio, sixteen hours later, Carol had touched down here in San Paulo. Nilda had called friends and arranged for them to meet her at the airport, but they were nowhere to be seen.

CHAPTER TWO

Just then Carol's mind popped back to her present dilemma and as she opened her eyes, she saw the young, blonde haired lad that had been holding the sign approaching her.

"Are you Carol Perry?" He blurted out.

"Yes I am," was her reply.

"My parents are looking for you, but they thought that Nilda said your name was Nancy."

By then the parents came running up apologizing for the mistake and hugging and reassuring Carol that all was well.

"We are Carol and Calvin Nelson, Missionaries from the United States here in San Paulo, and this is our son Troy. When we didn't find you right away, we thought that you had been kidnapped so we called the Federal Police. They are on their way here now to investigate."

"Oh Praise the Lord," exclaimed Carol as a huge wave of relief came over her.

"Will you come to our house and rest and relax until it's time for your plane to leave?"

"Oh, I would be glad to," Said Carol, so relieved to be accepted. Carol went with them to their home where they fixed her a good hot meal and visited with her until it was time to get back on the plane. The Nelsons stayed until they saw Carol safely on the plane. They were still waiving as the plane taxied away from the terminal.

It was a very small plane and as Carol looked around, she suddenly realized there were only a couple other passengers who obviously couldn't speak English. Carol pulled a book out of her purse and tried not to look nervous, but it was not a pleasant experience. She kept looking out the small window at the jungle below. It was a huge relief when she finally saw the airport come into view. It was a tiny airport as Londrina was just a small village. The plane rolled to a stop and the attendants opened the door to a down ramp.

At the bottom of the stair was the most beautiful sight. It was Nilda with a little brown baby in a beautiful white shawl in her arms. Carol almost ran down the stairs. Nilda put the precious little bundle in Carol's arms and gave her a big hug.

"I am so glad you finally made it here," said Nilda, "I was so scared that something had happened to you."

"It was a terrible experience but this makes it all worth it," Carol said as she looked down at the baby in her arms. She just kept crying and hugging and kissing the beautiful little baby, who was now ten days old by the time Carol finally got to her.

"I have a taxi waiting out front," said Nilda, "lets get you to our home."

Carol barely heard what Nilda was saying, as she was in another world, cooing and clicking her tongue at the beautiful baby in her arms.

The taxi pulled up in front of Nilda's residence and they

got out. There was a large iron gate and a huge stone fence

surrounding the place. It was a tiny house by our

standards, but just an average house by local standards.

Nilda took Carol to a small kitchen, introduced her to her

husband, and asked her if she would like some coffee.

"I love coffee," Carol said, not knowing what she was

getting into. Nilda came with a tiny cup half the size of

what she was used to at home, the coffee was so strong and

so thick that it would grow hair on your arm, but Carol

choked it down and learned very quickly not to ask for

seconds.

"Tell us about yourself," said Nilda,

"What brought you here to adopt this child?"

"Well," Carol began, "I guess it started when I was a little

child. I was born into a very loving and close family with

three older brothers, one younger brother and one older

sister. That was fine for a couple years but then our Mother was taken from us and things really got difficult. Well meaning friends and family didn't think my dad could take care of all of us so they were always trying to split us up. Dad was determined, however, and he would not let them. My sister Carmen had to step up and be the woman of the house. Between her and I we did the house cleaning and the laundry and helped dad with the cooking, and I must admit that the house was always clean, we had clean clothes to wear, although somewhat washed out at times, and we always had something to eat. In the evenings Dad would gather us around the piano and he would play the violin, Carmen would play the piano and we would all sing. Anyway I learned a deep appreciation for family and I couldn't wait until I could have a family of my own. I also developed a deep love for children. I would babysit for people every chance I got. I would even babysit for free just to be around the kids. When dad was taken from us, I was just a teenager. My oldest brother, Leon tried to keep the family together, even though he was trying to put himself through college at the time. There were many uneasy moments during this time as I never knew for sure where I would be sleeping that night. Sometimes I would stay at Leon's and sometimes I would stay with my cousin Janet or some other friend. Loran and I started dating when we were barely in high school. I loved school but I was always looking forward to the time when I could be married and start my own family. During the summer of my junior year, Loran and I were driving around and had my cousin Janet and another cousin with us. We girls started fooling around pulling on the steering wheel while he was driving. He ended up getting a ticket for reckless driving and so his parents forbid that he and I should see each other. As a result of this, instead of me finishing high school and Loran starting college, we ran away and got married.

After a brief stay in North Dakota, we came back to Bruce where Loran ran a Television Repair shop and started college. As our family began to grow we moved to Brookings and started our business called Perry Electric. During the next twenty years I gave birth to nine healthy babies. Doug is our firstborn; He is married and lives in California. He works in computers. Keven was born a year and one half later, he is married and lives in Brookings and works for his dad in his electrical business. Laurie was born three years later, and she is presently going to college in Brookings. Bryan was born the next year and he also works for his dad in the electrical business, Pam, born three years later has just finished high school and has a job in town, another four years brought Tonya who is in high school and helps her mom at home, plus she has a part time job after school. Three more years brought us Joel who is in junior high, four years younger is Tricia in grade school and finally Nathan who is just a toddler. I was so blessed to be able to be a stay at home mom and raise them, but I was always looking for ways to help other children. About ten years ago my husband and I decided to sponsor a child through an organization called World Vision. That was so fulfilling that I started thinking about adopting. I never dreamed it would bring me this far. Nilda smiled and gave Carol a big hug, then she took her to her room which was small with a little bed in the corner. She didn't have a crib, just a little carrier for the baby to sleep in. As Carol went to lie down on the bed she looked up at the cold concrete wall. She leaped up again as she watched a small green lizard crawling up the wall.

"Help somebody!" She cried, as she cringed against the opposite wall. Nilda came running, picked the lizard up and smiled.

"Don't worry," she said, "they are harmless." Carol was less than comforted by that and lay there staring at the wall the whole night.

After leaving Carol at the airport, Loran had returned to Brookings to busy himself with the daily aspects of living. Fortunately school was out so Pam and Tonya could juggle their job schedules to be home with Tricia and Nathan. It was a busy season at Perry Electric and Loran was struggling to keep up with the work load. He very was thankful for Keven and Bryan and his Brother Bob who were keeping things going and on track. With the girls taking care of things at home he was able to work a full day on the job except when he was on the phone trying to run ahead of Carol.

The next day, Nilda had Carol up early, not that she slept much anyway, but they boarded a bus and were off to Kurtecheba, a nearby city, similar to a county seat in the United States. They got off at the Federal Police Building. When Nilda told the man in charge why they were there, he looked at Carol, then at the baby, scowled, and basically said in Portuguese, "Why in the world would anyone come all this way just to adopt a baby?" He was not very helpful. The building they needed to be at was across town, so Nilda convinced a policeman to take them there in his vehicle. The vehicle turned out to be more like an armored car than a police car, but they went across town and everyone got out of the way. The court officer was even more negative than the police, because he made fun of Carol for what she was doing.

"Let's go in the other room and pray," said Nilda. She went to a telephone to call her brother who was a lawyer and had his office not too far away.

"You pray," said Nilda, "I'll be right back." A few minutes later, she came back with a paper in her hand, and they went back in to see the court officer. She calmly laid the paper in front of the belligerent man and stepped back. As the man started reading, his face turned pale and his whole mood changed. He started smiling and cooing at the baby, he even got down on his knees and made faces to get the baby to smile. You can only guess what was on that paper but it certainly changed his attitude. He immediately signed the necessary papers. It still took a couple days to get all the paperwork done because things just don't move that fast there in such a remote area of Brazil. Nilda knew a Mennonite couple in town and they stayed with them. Carol was able to communicate with them a little by singing songs that they both knew. When they finally got all the paperwork done, they were on their way back to San Paulo.

Back at Nilda's that evening, it was dusk and a chill was in the air. Carol heard a banging on the gate outside, and cautiously peeked out to see what was going on. She saw a young girl, scantily dressed and shivering in the chilly evening. She had a raspy cough that sounded terrible. Carol grabbed the only flannel shirt she had with her and tossed it over the fence to her and she disappeared into the night. Nilda came out and said scoldingly, "you shouldn't have done that, tomorrow night the street will be full with beggars."

Meanwhile in Brookings, the Immigration service had contacted Loran and told him that they needed a certified copy of his marriage license and his birth certificate. Because he had been born in Hamlin County, he had go all the way over to Hayti South Dakota to the court house there to get his birth certificate, then dash madly to Pipestone Minnesota where he and Carol were married, then frantically head for Minneapolis. Loran walked into the INS office at five minutes to five with the papers and then drove all the way back home.

Later that evening the phone rang and Loran knew it was Carol. "Walk outside and look at the moon," she said, "Let's pray together looking at the same moon. I have Kalee with me and I'm ready to come home." It was an awesome moment, both of them praying on the phone and looking at the same moon even though they were thousands of miles apart. As Loran stared at the moon his mind wandered momentarily to a less stressful time when he was just a lad on the farm in the dead of winter and in the full of the moon after nine o'clock in the evening he and his brothers would grab their sleds and head out to the pasture.

It was so still, crisp and peaceful the snow just sparkled in the bright moonlight. No flashlights were needed as they could see very clearly to maneuver their sleds down their favorite hill. Loran's dream bubble popped as abruptly as it had begun.

"I will call Jan at Travel One in the morning and get things going," he said. That proved to be more of a challenge than he anticipated. Trying to book a flight out of a small town in the heart of Brazil was not an easy thing to do. He ended up with two choices and he made the wrong one. He booked her on a small local airline that wasn't dependable. It was a little sixteen passenger plane with no frills. Carol boarded the plane and it took off out over the jungle. Almost immediately it ran into bad weather and for several hours she watched out the window as they skimmed above the tree tops, tossing violently at times.

It was during this time that Janet got a premonition that Carol was in trouble so she called the prayer chain and they all began to pray earnestly for Carol.

There were only a few passengers on the plane and a young man named Amedico came and sat by her to help her with the baby. Kalee's milk had gone sour and she had a bad tummy ache. Amedico could only speak a few words of English but they managed to communicate by sign language. They both breathed a huge sigh of relief when they landed in Rio. The young boy decided to stay with Carol until she got through customs and found her flight. It was a short lived rejoicing that they experienced because bad news was waiting for them when they got to customs. Carol handed her papers to the man and he got a solemn look on his face as he said, "These are not original documents, they are only copies. You have to have the originals."

Carol was devastated. She didn't know what to do or where to turn. She knew God had sent her here and He wouldn't give up on her now. She turned to Amedico, "Parents," she said, "Can you take me to your parents?" Amedico looked confused for a moment.

"mia and pia" Carol said gesturing wildly, "home."

Amedico's face lit up, "Ah" he said, "my parents, I'll take you to my home."

He flagged down a taxi and helped Carol get in with the baby. He gave directions to the cab driver. The driver scowled and shrugged his shoulders. He put the cab in gear and they were off down the narrow street. As they drove along the street got narrower and rougher. The cab would hit a huge pot hole, and would lurch almost out of control, the driver would curse and drive even faster. Each area they came into seemed darker and more foreboding and Carol prayed harder and harder for guidance as to what to do.

Suddenly Amedico said, "Turn in here."

The cab driver swerved into the driveway. It was a small

village with no electricity, and no phones. They drove up

to a small structure made of cement block with tiny

windows. Carol gave the driver some money, and he left.

Amedico went inside and came back out and said, "This is

my mother's house but she is not home." He disappeared

as Carol walked nervously back and forth on the porch. It

was a hot sticky evening and very uncomfortable. Alone

and panic stricken she looked up, "God you didn't bring me

all this way for this, there has to be a way. You know I

can't leave the baby here." Soon a car drove up and

Amedico jumped out and helped Carol and the baby in the

car. "Pastor," Carol said, "Church." Amedico shook his

head and drove off again down the bumpy road. He turned

into a yard with a big iron gate and a lot of old buildings

with people all over, some in wheelchairs and some very

handicapped.

Carol said under her breath, "Oh Lord! What is happening,

why are we here?"

Amedico got out of the car and took the baby and said

"follow me." They went up a flight of stairs and he opened

the door. It was as if they had stepped into another world,

the room was so bright and cheerful. Inside sat the pastor

and his wife, and their two teenage daughters. The girl's

faces lit up when they saw the baby and they ran to

Amedico.

"Oh, let me have the baby," one exclaimed, "she it so

cute."

"Her milk is sour in her bottle, Carol said, "Do you have

any fresh milk?" The girls looked with a blank look at

Amedico.

"Leichy" said Amedico. One girl ran to get the milk, she filled the bottle and put it in Kalee's mouth. Almost immediately Kalee settled down. Amedico began to explain Carol's problem to the pastor so he could help decide what to do.

They called the airlines and found out that there was one flight out in the morning and it was the last one available for a few days. Carol knew she had to be on it because she was running out of money. By now she had been there over three weeks. She called Nilda and explained the problem to her. It was decided that Carol would have to leave Kalee with these strangers and head home. She left money with the pastor to have Nilda flown to Rio to pick up Kalee and take her back to Londrina while she worked on getting the right papers.

The next morning was a heart wrenching parting as Carol put her precious baby in the arms of a stranger and walked

51

away. They had a young boy drive Carol to the airport. She checked in and went and sat down where she thought she was supposed to wait. The next thing she saw was a bunch of people rushing to a different door. She jumped up and ran and just barely got through the door before it closed or she would have missed her flight.

It was a sad reunion when Carol arrived at the Sioux Falls Airport the next day. Loran tried to console her and let her know that she had done the right thing by coming home, but she felt like she had failed. They immediately started planning their strategy for getting Kalee home. Carol called Nilda the next day to make sure that she had gotten back to Londrina all right with the baby.

"I am so sorry that I got the wrong papers," said Nilda, "I will call my brother, the lawyer and have him go back to the Federal palace to straighten it out. The baby is doing fine and we will take good care of her."

CHAPTER THREE

The children were all happy to have their mother home, especially two year old Nathan, but they too were very disappointed not to have their new sister there.

Carol continued to call Nilda and the news was not good. Her brother got new papers made but they needed to be signed by the birth mother. Not only was she illiterate, but she disappeared into the night a few minutes after she left the baby. Now the problem was not with the Brazilian officials. They were willing to let her out of the country but it was with INS in Minneapolis. There was a stern old man in charge who would not budge. Again Carol called the prayer chain and put it to prayer. The next day Carol and Loran were back in Minneapolis and found out that they needed several documents translated right away. They called the professional translating services and they told them it would take at least two weeks to get what they needed. They went back to the car and prayed and called the foreign language department of the local college. A pleasant young lady gave them an address of a student who said he could do it right away. They started driving and couldn't find the way so they stopped a policeman. He said, "I know where that is, follow me," so they had police escort right to the place. They thanked the policeman and hurried inside where the young man was waiting. He said, "this won't take long," and began to translate. When he was done Loran handed him fifty dollars and they dashed off to the immigration office. They arrived with just a few minutes to spare. Walking in expecting to talk to the same grumpy old man, They were surprised to find a nice young man who explained that his boss had gone on vacation and now they needed to get the new papers from Nilda in his hands in the next two days. Overjoyed, Carol and Loran hugged each other. But their joy faded quickly when they asked themselves, "How are we going get papers from a remote area in Brazil to Minneapolis that quick?"

"God will make a way," Carol firmly replied as she was dialing Nilda's number.

"This may be a strange coincidence," said Nilda, "But there is a man here who is flying to Minneapolis tomorrow. He says it will only cost him forty dollars extra to go get the papers and deliver them to INS.

"They will be at the INS office before they close tomorrow night."

Carol took down his name and address and Loran immediately sent him a check for forty dollars. Carol called INS the next afternoon and the papers were there. A week later their letter with the forty dollar check was returned "no such person, no such address." The phantom stranger was obviously an angel dispatched by God in

answer to the fervent prayers of the prayer chain. The Bible
says that angels are ministering spirits sent to minister to
the needs of God's people. Now all that Carol and Loran
had to do was to figure out how to get their daughter home.
They had a good friend in Florida whose husband worked
for the airline so she could fly anywhere in the country for
ten dollars. She would often fly to South Dakota just to
pick up some Shaklee products from Carol which was
cheaper than she could ship them, so they knew if they
could get Kalee to the United States, their friend would
bring her on home. So Loran bought Nilda another ticket
to Rio where he hired a stewardess to escort Kalee to
Miami so she could be picked by the friend.

Almost three weeks had passed by the time they got all this
together, so when the day finally arrived for their precious
little bundle to travel, The whole family was all on edge
and uptight with anticipation. Nilda called and reported

that she had delivered Kalee to the stewardess and watched

her get on the plane, so all the family could do was sit by

the phone and wait. When the phone rang it was not

exactly what they expected. It was the customs officer at

the Miami airport saying that he had a baby sitting on his

desk with Carol's name on her and he wondered what we

wanted him to do with her. Carol and Loran looked at each

other and panic filled their voices as they frantically tried to

call their friend but could not get hold of her. This was in a

day before cell phones. They had never had such a helpless

feeling. About that time the phone rang again and it was

the friend.

"I'm in the airport," she said, "I can see the baby through

the fence but they won't let me through the gate to get her

because I don't have a passport." After about a half an hour

of Haggling she convinced them to call us back and get

permission to hand Kalee over to her. She was pretty well

57

frazzled by then, but she was still able to catch her flight. A few hours later she was coming down the ramp at Sioux Falls airport to the cheers and excitement of the Perry family. What a homecoming it was!

Kalee was such a chubby little bundle of joy that she settled right into the family routine and the big sisters squabbled over who was going to take care of her.

In August Kalee wasn't even three months old yet, but Loran and Carol had earned a trip to a Shaklee convention in San Francisco so there was only one thing to do, they had to take her along. They had a grand time, they got to see their oldest son, Doug who lived in California, and he got to see his new baby sister. When they got to their hotel Carol hadn't slept for two days and she was hungry so Loran ordered a breakfast from room service. It's a good thing that he took a picture of her eating because the next morning she wouldn't believe that it really happened.

CHAPTER FOUR

It was Fall again, Pam had gotten married, Kalee was barely six months old, and one day the phone rang. "Hello" said Carol. "Mrs. Perry, this Nancy from IAAA, you have a new baby girl." Carol almost dropped the phone. "But I thought the India program was at a standstill."

"Well, it's moving and your name came up. Your baby was born six weeks ago but we couldn't call you because it was a day to day struggle to see if she was going to survive."

"So is she alright," Carol asked.

"She is a fighter." Nancy exclaimed, "She has made it against all odds, and her health is basically good as far as we can tell. Of course you know how we get these babies. Young girls come in on the train probably seven months along, go to this place they call a clinic where this man they call a doctor gives them a drug, they deliver and get back on the train. The "doctor" puts the baby in a garbage bag and throws it out the back door. We come along and tap the toes to see which ones are still alive and take them back to try to save them."

"But we went to Brazil," Carol started.

"I'm sure after reading your home study that you can handle this one too," said Nancy reassuringly. So the scurry began to get a second crib in the nursery and prepare the family for yet another member. The girls were very excited. Although she was born in late November, it was March before Lexi arrived home. When Carol named her they asked her to give Lexi an India middle name so she chose Asha which means hope. How fitting because she had no hope until the Perrys came along.

Thankfully, they did not have to travel to India to pick Lexi up, but rather she was escorted with a group of babies all the way to Minneapolis. The agency then hired a stewardess to bring her to the Sioux Falls airport. When she came down the ramp with Lexi in her arms, she was crying, although the flight was only an hour long she had so bonded with her that she couldn't bear to give her up. As they opened the blankets to get their first look at her, Carol and Loran couldn't help but be shocked. Although they thought they had prepared themselves for this, because they knew she was a seventh month abortion, and that her birth mother was a very young girl, still they could not believe what they saw. She was so tiny and shriveled and her skin was like leather, at four months old, weighing five pounds and eight ounces, she looked so pitiful. But it was love at first sight as the kids all crowded around to touch and hold her.

When they got her home they started filling her with good

nutrition including a lot of Shaklee products, but her little digestive system was not well developed and everything gave her tummy aches. The only thing that would relieve them was to crush papaya tablets, dissolve them in water, and feed them to her. Then Loran would prop her on his hip, squeeze her little tummy in the crook of his elbow, and walk the floor. This is what Loran did for many, many hours in those first few months. Gradually she began to sleep at night, her skin softened up and she began to fill out into a beautiful little girl. Her and Kalee became the best of buddies, they would sit and giggle at each other but Carol had to watch them closely because Kalee , only five months older, was so much bigger that she would sit on Lexi.

So how do child ten and child eleven make it in a large family? Even though Carol was a stay at home mom she couldn't be everywhere at once so just as Laurie took over

Tricia and mothered her, Tonya took over Kalee and Tricia took over Lexi and everyone knew their responsibilities. That's the way it is in a large family, and it seems to be a good thing. What better way to teach responsibility.

Sure enough, just as she said, in May Deb brought Grandma and Grandpa their first granddaughter. They named her Amanda and she started life with aunt Kalee and aunt Lexi being about the same age as she.

Carol and Loran had to admit that it was a challenge being a new parent and a new grandparent at the same time, but the girls became the best of friends and many times they were in the same activities. It was fun for Carol and Loran to see people's reaction when they would point out that one girl was their daughter and the other was their granddaughter.

For the next couple years the older girls dressed Kalee and Lexi like kewpie dolls, took care of them and spoiled them.

In order for the girls to get their citizenship, Carol and Loran had to go to Sioux Falls and go before the Federal judge to get them naturalized. When the ceremony was over the judge stepped down in his robe and asked, "May I hold the girls?" He held Kalee and she grinned real big for him. Then he no more than put Lexi on his shoulder than she vomited all over him. He thought it was pretty funny.

It was one day in nineteen eighty three Carol said, "You know we are not getting and younger, if we are going to get another child we had better start soon."

"Lord help me," Loran said under his breath, "I've mortgaged everything I own to get these two." But, the next day Carol was on the phone to Nancy at IAAA putting her name in for a boy from India. So began the process all over again, sending documents to the Indian consulate, to Immigration service, and to the agency. They had some trouble getting documents through the Indian Consulate which was located in Chicago.. They could not afford to travel to Chicago but thankfully Loran's brother Wayne lived there and he stepped in to help them and went to the consulate and pushed them on through. What a blessing to have the support of family. When that was all done they began the waiting period again. Summer nineteen eighty four arrived and they had heard nothing. Carol called the agency and heard Nancy say, "Oh Mrs. Perry, you have to realize there are dozens of people ahead of you."

"Oh but did you remember this is a ministry, and we are just following Matthew 25:35, I was a stranger and you took me in," was Carol's reply.

It wasn't but a few weeks later Carol got the call,

"Mrs. Perry, your new son is ready to travel."

Again Carol had to search for an India name so she ended up with Dallas Sunil.

"Praise God for credit cards," said Loran," I know they can be a curse, but the banker would not lend me any more money so I will have to max out the credit cards to get Dallas home." He figured they would be paying on them the rest of their lives but they had to believe it was worth it because they had invested their whole lives in saving these three children.

The day arrived when Dallas would be traveling and they found out that he was being escorted by a young boy along with four other high risk infants, all the way from Calcutta to Minneapolis. They were a little apprehensive, but everything went fine except Dallas' papers got lost along the way, so what little they would have known about him was gone. That happened to Lexi as well so they were not really surprised. Just like Lexi they had a stewardess bring Dallas to the Sioux Falls airport. When they got him he looked like a shriveled up little prune at three pounds and two ounces. They had brought the whole family along to the airport so they had taken the motor home. When they all got back in the motor home Pam said, "I want to hold him on the way home." So Pam sat on the davenport and took Dallas on her lap. They had gotten only a few miles up the interstate when Pam yelled, "Mom I think there is something wrong with him, he's not breathing!" Carol jumped up grabbed him and shook him. Dallas gasped and started to breathe a little.

"We've got to get him to the clinic right away," Carol shouted.

"If there are any patrolmen watching we will just have to explain," Loran said as he jammed the pedal to the floor. He didn't know the old rig could go that fast but they made it to Brookings and rushed right into the clinic and took him to Dr. Patterson. He gave them some medicine a told them to watch him close which they surely did. To help watch him closely included a breathing monitor which he had to sleep with for the next several months. They also started him on all the Shaklee products they could get down him.

Now Carol and Loran's family was an even dozen and they settled down to raising them and paying the bills, but the enemy was not willing to let them alone

CHAPTER FIVE

It had actually started many years earlier when at a young age Loran realized he was being called by God for some special assignment. It was in the time he spent alone on the farm that he began to feel that God had something special in mind for him, but how could he talk to anyone about it without sounding arrogant, and growing up in the Methodist church he had never heard of a person having a call from God on their life. But I Kings 19 says that God doesn't come in the wind, the earthquake, or the fire but with a still small voice. At the same time as he began to feel the call of God on his life, it seemed that traumatic things began to happen as though some evil force was trying to get rid of him. John 16:33 declares, "In this world you will have trouble, but be of good cheer I have overcome the world."

It was a warm summer day and six year old Loran was

playing in the loft of the garage as he often did. There was

a window at the top of the stairs and as he came up those

stairs, a large bumble bee buzzing in the window startled

him. He jumped back instinctively and fell all the way to

the cement floor below and landed on his head. The next

thing he remembered was laying out in the yard on his

favorite blue blanket cradled in his mom's arms while she

was showing him the fresh eggs she had just gathered in

her apron. Loran came out of it with a huge knot on his

head but apparently no other injury.

Another time Loran's cousin Bryce was visiting and he had

just gotten a bow and arrows for Christmas and they were

taking turns shooting the arrows through an upper window

in the granary while the other person would wait in the

granary to pick up the arrows. Well, Loran was in the

granary and nothing was happening so he peaked out the

window and wham! An arrow hit him right in the forehead,

just missing his eye by an inch. He got a huge black and blue bump on his forehead but no permanent damage.

When Loran became a teenager, again his cousin Bryce was visiting for the summer and a warm summer evening found them looking for something to do, and Bryce said," Lets take the old hot rod for a drive." The "old hot rod," was an old nineteen thirty Chevrolet with the body stripped off.

"I'll drive," said Harold, another visiting cousin, He was only twelve years old but of course South Dakota didn't even have driver's licenses yet at that time, and farm kids always drove when they were very young. They took off down the gravel road. Bryce was in the passenger seat and Loran was sitting on the back deck. That vehicle without its body was very light on the back end. As they were passing the neighbor's hog farm, Loran got the bright idea to start jumping up and down on the back to see if he could make it bounce. It began to bounce alright, so much so that Harold lost control and they went into the ditch at about thirty five miles per hour. Loran flew off and landed on his side skidding down the ditch bank. The bumper caught the fence and tore a big hole in it, allowing the pigs to escape. The hot rod didn't have a windshield but one of the side posts remained. It caught the barbed wire and stretched it. If it hadn't the wire would have caught Bryce right in the neck. The three cousins walked home to get Loran's dad and confess what they had done. He was so angry that he made them go back and round up the pigs and repair the fence before he would take Loran to the hospital to get checked out. As it turned out Loran had a broken wrist and severe bruises all down his leg that stayed with him the rest of the summer. He had to start school that fall with his arm in a cast and unable to write. Again the book of Proverbs chapter 22:15 says, "Foolishness is bound up in the heart of a child but the rod of correction will drive it far from him." Loran gained a whole lot of wisdom about being foolish that summer.

One of the chores on the farm that went along with milking the cows was to spray them down with fly spray so the flies would leave them alone enough so they would stand still while they were milked. It was customary to use a hand pump sprayer to accomplish that task and It worked quite well, though a little tedious. Loran's brother Dale was working in a body shop that summer, and he brought home an electric spray gun.

"Hey" said Bryce, "why couldn't we fill the spray gun with fly spray, get an extension cord and use it to spray the cows?"

"It should work just fine," Loran said," but first we have to fix the switch in the handle, it doesn't seem to be working right." So the two cousins proceeded to tear the gun apart and repair the switch but they forgot to put one little piece of insulation back in as they reassembled it. Standing on the dry garage floor it worked great so they took it to the barn where Loran was holding it in his hands and standing on the damp floor of the milking area. Bryce plugged it in and Loran got the full blast of current. His hand froze to the handle so of course, he couldn't let go of it. He was screaming at the top of his lungs or so it seemed to him, but in fact Bryce couldn't hear him standing right next to him. It seemed like forever before Bryce realized there was something wrong and kicked the sprayer out of Loran's hand. This was the third time the forces of evil had tried to take Loran out before God's purpose for his life could be realized.

During threshing season that year Loran was hauling bundles with a team of horses on a hayrack. It was always a challenge to see who could come in with the tallest load.

He had his piled especially high that afternoon. He was kind of proud of it as he threw his pitchfork up on top and crawled way up there for the ride in from the field. On the way in, the wagon went through a little dip and made a loud creaking noise, it spooked the horses, they jumped to the side and over went his load with Loran scrambling to stay on top of it. As he picked himself up from the ground, a wave of thankfulness went over him as he looked down to see his pitchfork jammed in the ground right along side of him. Once again he had narrowly missed being taken out by the destroyer.

Several weeks after that it was corn picking season and Loran's Dad was using a pull type picker with the wagon being pulled along side as it went down the field. It was Loran's job to bring empty wagons out to him and exchange with him so Loran could haul the corn to the crib. Loran was waiting at the end of the field and as his dad approached he could see that the wagon was getting full and needed leveling. Loran jumped from the tractor and ran down the corn row toward the wagon, but instead of approaching from the side, He ran straight toward it, intending to jump up on the front to level the corn. As he jumped his foot slipped and went right down under the wheel. In an instant he was on the ground and the tire of the wagon ran full length over his body. Loran remembered just having time to turn his head and put his hands over his face as the wheel went over him. His dad was quite relieved to see him get up and walk away from that one. Loran was in bed that night before his Mother heard about the mishap. She came up and woke him up to examine him. All she found was a bruise on his thigh where he had a jack knife in his pocket. Once again he had eluded the enemy.

As Loran entered his senior year at Bruce high school that

fall, he decided to join the National Guard. There were no big wars going on, it was a chance to make a few bucks, and it was macho. Besides Loran's older brother, Wayne was already a sergeant in the local unit. Loran thought that would be a good thing but found out later that it wasn't all good. When Wayne became an officer he would give the sergeants a nasty job and they would turn around and take it out on Loran, and big brother was very careful not to show any favoritism. To Loran, it seemed like a safe time to be in the military but again that evil one who was trying to take him out was lurking.

It was a hot sultry August afternoon at summer camp in Camp McCoy Wisconsin. The firing range had a pit underneath the targets where targets were pulled up and down and marked for scoring. It faced west and boy! Was it hot down there! All the guys had their helmets off trying to stay cool. The line officer came through and said, "Get those blankity-blank helmets on or you'll all be on KP tomorrow!" No sooner had Loran secured his helmet and the bullets started flying overhead. The target frames were made of thin pieces of steel and the chances of a bullet hitting them was very small but the next thing Loran heard was a whiz and a clank and a riochet came off the frame and hit him right on top of the head. Needless to say, no one took their helmets off the rest of the day. Loran picked up the slug and matched it to the dent in his helmet and he still has it among his memorabilia.

It was sometime later that fall of his senior year that Loran and Carol were "cruising" around Bruce on a Saturday evening in his little blue thirty seven Chevy coupe. After while when they had been up and down each street at least twice they decided stop and chat on a dark street nicknamed "lovers lane" Loran left the motor running because it was chilly. What he didn't realize was that his muffler had a leak in it and the next thing Carol remembered was Loran falling against the door handle and rolling out on the ground. She dizzily crawled out after him but he was stiff as a board. She had never heard of CPR or mouth to mouth resuscitation but perhaps she invented it that night. Somehow she revived him even though she was almost unconscious herself. He recovered with no after effects except to this day he has a very low tolerance to carbon monoxide. Once again the enemy struck a near fatal blow to this young couple.

On July twenty sixth nineteen sixty, Loran had been in Brookings working and was on his way back home to Bruce. The sun was still high in the afternoon sky as he turned off of Highway fourteen and headed up the road to Bruce. As he approached the first intersection, a cloud of dust off to the west caught his attention. A car was bearing down on the intersection at a high rate of speed.

"There's a stop sign there," Loran thought to himself, "he is going to stop. He will stop I know he's going to stop. Oh no, he's not stopping!" Loran jammed the accelerator to the floor of his little maroon fifty two Ford. The little flat head v-8 leaped forward with all the power it could muster, but it wasn't enough to get him out of the path of the big blue Plymouth that was bearing down from the West. As Loran entered the intersection, his speed was in excess of seventy miles per hour. The on coming car t-boned him right in the driver's side door. It was all over in a few seconds, but it seemed like an eternity. The little Ford rolled several times side ways, down the ditch bank. Then it struck the barbed wire fence. There were no seat belts, of course, so as the car struck the fence Loran was apparently hanging out the windshield cavity, and was raked on his neck and down his back by the barbs. Next the fence caught the car and it began flipping end over end out across the field like a rock skipping on the water. The field having been freshly plowed, was soft and probably saved Loran's life but it sure raised a cloud of dust. After the seeming eternity when everything stopped and the dust settled, the car was resting on its top and Loran was sitting through the windshield hole with the car on his lap. Were it not for the soft ground his legs would certainly have been crushed. As the dead silence closed in around him, Loran's first thought was, "Oh thank God I'm all in one piece." Then he heard an ominous gurgling sound and felt something warm and sticky oozing around his waist.

"Oh no I'm bleeding to death!" was his next frantic thought. Then he put his hand down into the sticky ooze and brought it back up to his face. Suddenly he realized it was anti freeze from the engine. What a warm feeling of relief swept over him.

About that time passers by had stopped and came running out to the car. Three times they tried to lift the car off of Loran's legs and dropped it again.

"Hey," he shouted, "Wait a minute." He began frantically digging in the soft dirt with his hands. Shortly he had enough removed to drag himself out from under the wreck. With a severely bruised shin Loran limped back to the road where he found the other driver, a young boy who had borrowed his grandmother's car without permission and taken it for a joy ride, was sitting on the ditch bank laughing. They wouldn't let Loran at him or it's hard to tell what would have happened. Obviously he was in shock because when the ambulance arrived he was bawling like a baby. They put him in back and Loran sat up front with the driver.

Carol was out walking with the children when they tried to reach her so they called Loran's dad and he found her coming down the sidewalk near her house. When he told her that Loran had been in a car accident she fainted. Fortunately she had a friend with her who grabbed the baby as she fell.

Anyone who looked at the car could not believe how anyone ever got out alive from the wreck. Looking at it himself Loran could not believe it either, but it gave him an eerie feeling because he new that something supernatural was happing here and if he wanted to stay ahead of the destroyer who was obviously out to get him, he would have to respond to God's gentle nudging if He was to continue to protect him. Proverbs 3:25 admonishes us, "Do not be afraid of sudden terror nor of trouble from the wicked when it comes, for the Lord will be your confidence and will keep your foot from being caught."

While working at Sand's Electric, a friend and fellow worker got a moonlighting job at the Flandreau Indian

School and asked Loran to help him. They were working in the hallway of one of the dormitories when Loran climbed an eight foot ladder and crawled onto a large metal air duct. Fortunately he kept one foot on the top of the ladder. He cut into a wire with a cutter that had defective insulation on the handle and his hand immediately froze to the cutter. As the current went through his body the best way he could describe it was that it was like looking out the back window of a car going really fast. Everything was going away from him at a tremendous rate of speed. The only thing he could do was to kick the ladder out from under his one foot, so he kicked with all his might. Down he came with tools flying everywhere. It was not a graceful landing but he was very grateful to be alive.

One cold winter evening Loran made a very foolish decision to go riding snowmobile alone at night. He often went riding alone because he really didn't have a riding partner, but alone on a cold dark night was not a good combination. About five miles out of town he was running high on the ditch bank right close to the asphalt. Buried in the snow was a bead ring from a truck tire. A bead ring is a metal ring about two feet in diameter. When his skis went over it, it tipped up and caught the exhaust pipe and his sled became airborne, he landed in the middle of the road, while the snowmobile came to rest in a huge snow bank in the ditch. With a black snowmobile suit on and lying on the black asphalt, if he would have been knocked out an oncoming driver would have little chance to see him in time. His head had hit the asphalt so hard that he had flecks of helmet paint inside his goggles but the helmet did its job. He pulled the snowmobile from the snow bank and found that it was still drivable, so he was able to make it back to town.

Another winter, with the help of his uncle Walter, Loran had just finished building a bucket truck for the electric business. It was kind of a risky undertaking, but coming from a do it yourself farm boy background, he had watched his older brothers do similar engineering feats at home on the farm. Loran had tested the thing out and it seemed to be working fine. There was a snowstorm that week and Loran heard that his brother Wayne needed some snow removed from the roof of one of his apartment buildings. That seemed like quite a challenge because the eves were about twenty five feet up. He went up and was pulling the snow down just fine when he needed to move a little. He hit the controls and the unit bounced once and the upper cylinder folded up and Loran, bucket and all came crashing down. He had made up his mind ahead of time that if it dropped he would crouch down in the bucket and ride it out. Well, that was fine but as he crouched down his back became exposed through the side opening in the bucket and as he came down his back struck a porch roof. The enemy had planned that he would be paralyzed on the spot but he was able to drive home. By that time his back was swollen from his neck to his butt. Carol rushed him to the clinic where they took X-rays. The doctor came back and said," you have the back bone of a teenager, go home and ice it. So the back healed, Loran reengineered the bucket truck, beefed up the cylinders, and life went on.

It was an ordinary work day and Joel was finishing a wiring project that needed Dad's expertise to help him so Loran was riding with Joel as they returned to town. As they approached the first stoplight the light turned yellow but Joel was way too close and traveling too fast to stop, so he took his foot off the accelerator intending to coast on through. From the other way was a new dark green Lincoln waiting to turn. Behind the wheel was a young girl who had just received her driver's license that afternoon and was taking her girlfriend out for a drive in her daddy's new Lincoln. She assumed that the yellow light was for her to complete her left hand turn, so she turned right in front of Joel. Unfortunately Loran was not wearing his seatbelt so his head broke the windshield, the rear view mirror destroyed his glasses, and his wrist wiped out the radio knob. By the time the ambulance got there Loran and Joel were out walking around to see if the girls were alright. Loran started to climb into the ambulance but the EMT made him lay down on the ground so they could put him on a board. The EMT was obviously new because he tried to put the neck brace on Loran backwards. When they got to the emergency room they kept pulling on Loran's arm to get him into position to x-ray his head to see if he had a concussion and he kept yelling because they were pulling on his wrist that he thought was broken. Well he came out with his badly bruised arm in a sling, his head bandaged with a concussion and had to get a new pair of glasses. Joel's truck was totaled.

Being an electrician, Traumatic occurrences were not that unusual. Once Loran was working on an irrigation controller for a friend when he thought he had cleared the short so instead of closing the door to turn it back on, he stuck his head in there and turned it on (duh!) and of course, it exploded in a huge fireball. Loran's eyebrows were singed and he had to wear dark glasses for several weeks, but again he escaped permanent injury. He had barely grown his eyebrows back when the little cab over pickup he was driving had a carburetor problem and caught on fire. The engine compartment was right beside him in the cab and as he opened the hood to see what was wrong the cab was immediately filled with fire. After several frantic grabs he found the door handle and fell out on the ground. He was uninjured but his eyebrows were completely gone again. Anyway In spite of what seemed to be relentless attacks from the destroyer it became apparent that the enemy was a defeated foe and he could have no more power in Loran's life than what power he gave him, A fact that he should have learned much earlier.

CHAPTER SIX

It was a chilly winter day and Carol had taken baby Dallas

and gone to visit her aunt Idella. They were sitting and

chatting while drinking coffee when Carol looked down

and noticed that Dallas was not breathing. She jumped up

screaming and Idella began to pray. As Carol balanced the

baby on one arm she grabbed the phone and dialed for help.

"Hello, help, send someone quick, my baby is dying!"

The ambulance crew responded immediately, but the streets

were glare ice so it still took quite sometime to arrive.

Meanwhile, Idella's prayer had been heard and was being

answered. Several years earlier God had prepared Carol for

this moment. She suddenly remembered the time her dog,

Poco was having puppies and one of them did not start

breathing. She had rushed it to the vet and the vet grabbed

it in both hands, lifted it high above his head and swung it downward in a quick sweeping motion. This action had saved the puppy's life and now Carol knew why she had witnessed it. In an unprecedented act of conviction and determination she took the baby firmly in both hands and lifted him high above her head and swung him downward while Idella looked on aghast. Dallas let out a squeak and began to breathe. It was several minutes later when the EMT came running in out of breath. When he heard what she had done he said, "Ma'am you definitely saved your son's life. We would not have gotten here in time!" Carol and Idella had a real praise session after that.

Carol and Loran were required to make regular reports to the agency on the progress of the children. This is a copy of a letter written by Loran on May third, nineteen eighty five.

Dear IAAA Staff:

We are so blessed with our son Dallas Sunil Perry. He will be eight months old on May Seventh. The time has gone so fast and in the six months we have had Dallas we have had many joys because of him.

Dallas' day starts about six or seven in the morning with a six ounce bottle of milk which he drinks really fast. It makes a guy hungry after sleeping all those hours. He goes back to sleep until about eight. Now brother, Nathan who is six and sleeps in the same room, carries him to the living room to watch a little TV. They also have a hollering session. Dallas loves to hear his own voice. Then along comes mom. It's bath time while the other kids get ready for school. After his bath he gets dressed and Oh what fun that is!

Now the kids are off to school and Dallas is hungry. He has a big bowl of cereal, his vitamins and more milk. No wonder he is gaining so fast. He is a whole sixteen pounds and gaining. A little short nap while mom gets Kalee and Lexi cleaned up. Now it's time to go for coffee, our everyday venture to the Staurolite Inn. The people there are like family. Dallas is whisked off to the kitchen, the dinning room or held by several people. He only has to give a look or a smile and everyone smiles back and loves him. Next a little nap on mom or dad's lap and it's time to go home. Mom has to get to work while Dallas plays either on the living room floor, in the playpen, or in his Johnny jump up. The little girls play well with him. Then I rock him to sleep. When he gets up he eats lunch which consists of one and one half jars of baby food and more milk. As you can tell, Dallas is a very healthy, happy baby.

As for mom and dad, we don't know what we would do without him. He is our son, truly a gift from God. Our lives have been so enriched by him. He responds to each of his family members. Tonya, who is seventeen, will be going away to school and she teases and says that she will take him with her. Joel, fourteen, combs Dallas' long dark hair and can't wait until he is old enough to ride three wheeler.

Tricia, ten, helps babysit him while I run errands. We have a lot of kids in our neighborhood who come over to play with Dallas.

Dallas' health is quite good, although he has had bronchitis, pneumonia, and earache. I take him to the clinic often to make sure he is OK. As of now, he is just fine. We expect some teeth soon because the drooling and biting on things. His disposition is super. His legs are strong from jumping in his Johnny jump up. He picks up objects and is able to hold his own bottle. He understands when spoken to, such as open your mouth, bye bye, hello, mamma, and much more. He can sit alone, and crawl around. He is doing everything he should for his age.

Respectfully;
Loran Perry
203 7th St. W
Brookings SD 57006

When the girls became preschool age Carol began checking

around and found out that there was an awesome preschool

program at the University.

"Lets enroll the girls in the college program," said Carol,

"It would be a great way to get them exposed to society and

to get people to interact with them."

"We are very fortunate to live in a town with a university,"

Loran replied, "There so many people up there from different cultures and countries that the kids won't stand out at all."

So Carol called the university and found out that space was limited in the program but the kids were able to get in and it turned out to be such a blessing to see the girls blossom out and grow and learn to interact with the other children. When it came time to enter kindergarten it made such a difference for them to have that preschool experience behind them. When Dallas was old enough he too was able to get in the college program and get the benefit of a head start. The university was actually glad to have the children because it was part of their program to teach child development and it was very helpful for their students to work with the kids.

Dallas developed a funny little quirk that kept his mom on

her toes, when he got tired, he would lay down wherever he was and go to sleep. One time it was in the sand box, one time on the sidewalk and one time in the closet.

One day Kalee was sitting on the floor in the bathroom watching her mother put on her makeup. "Take it off, take it off," exclaimed Kalee. Her mother looked down to see her rubbing the brown skin on her leg. "Oh honey!" exclaimed Carol, "God made you exactly like he wanted you and he doesn't make any mistakes."

"Well at least the bottoms of my feet are white," Kalee replied.

When Dallas was old enough to notice the difference in his skin Carol was praying with him as she was putting him to bed and he blurted out, "God I want to be white." So she went through the whole thing about how he was just the way God had planned for him to be. She thought it was done and as she was going out the door he turned his face to the wall and whispered, "But God I still want to be white!"

Another time Carol was praying with Dallas as she was putting him to bed and he was feeling scared so she said, 'You have nothing to worry about because God watches over you and He will be up all night."

"Dat not fair," replied Dallas.

Dallas had a lot of stomach trouble because he was born prematurely. The doctor recommended goat's milk because it was easier to digest. So the search began to find who in the area still had any goats. Loran had gotten goats' milk for Bryan when he was an infant from a farmer right outside of town, but he was long gone by now.

Today he could just type goat into Google but there was no internet yet. Loran finally called the Agriculture Department at the university and they gave him a name of a couple who lived by Wentworth about thirty miles away.

"Hey!, let's make it a family outing," said Loran, "Every body get in the car."

Forty minutes later they pulled into the farmyard of John and Karen Knutson. By the Barn were several black and white and brown and white goats looking with inquiring dark eyes through the fence. In a few moments the kids were all lined up by the fence petting the goats and scratching their ears.

"Hello sir," said Loran, reaching out his hand for a hearty handshake as Mr. Knutson came out of the house, "We have a young lad with stomach problems we are in desperate need of some goat's milk."

"Great," said Mr. Knutson, "You have come to the right place. We ship most of our milk to Chicago but we do sell quite a bit locally."

This started the relationship that lasted for several months and every week Loran would make the trip to Wentworth to get fresh goat's milk. Kalee and Lexi would often go along and got to know the Knutsons quite well, so well that the Knutsons asked if it would be alright to name a couple of their goats after them. Loran said "sure go ahead," even though the girls didn't think too much of it.

Grade school was an exciting time for Kalee as she really enjoyed learning and accomplishing things. She was and is somewhat of a perfectionist and loves excelling in whatever she is doing. Her teachers always loved her because of her willing attitude. Her mom and big sisters were always careful to have her dressed just right and her beautiful hair combed perfectly. Kalee developed many good friendships among her schoolmates but most of her friends were older than her because she always seemed older than her age. Lexi was a little more shy and clung to her mom but she did well in school and was accepted as a "little princess" where ever she went. Carol and Loran always referred to her as a princess because they never knew her background for sure, but they strongly suspected she actually might have royal blood because the people at the "orphanage" where she came from all called her "Princess Ruhma." One day when Lexi was about six or seven she had her neice, Amanda stay overnight and they were two giggly girls. Every thing was funny. In the morning they were trying to put honey from a squeeze bottle on their cereal and the honey was too thick and all they could get was a "pppfffsssttt" and then they would giggle. Soon they disappeared and didn't tell anyone where they were going.

"Has anyone seen the girls," said Carol?

"They are probably in the back yard," Loran said, "I will go check."

After checking the back yard, the basement, the rec room and the whole house, they began to get worried.

"I think we had better call the police," said Carol.

"Let's check the neighborhood first," Loran said, "I'm sure they are not too far away."

He started down the sidewalk past the little pink house where Cora DeGroot lived. Just then the two little runaways were coming out of Cora's house with fresh chocolate chip cookies in their hands.

"There you are!" Loran exclaimed, "Didn't you hear us yelling your names?"

"No we didn't hear anything," said Lexi, "We were in the basement with Cora."

"Why didn't you tell somebody where you were going," Loran said sternly.

"We were just out in the yard and Cora asked us if we wanted a cookie," said Amanda, "we didn't think anyone would care."

The family was all relieved to see them safely back in the

101

yard.

Mom wanted to keep the girls involved so she put them into soccer. Kalee did fairly well although she was not very excited about it, but poor Lexi she was so tiny she would just go out and stand on the field with her head down.

The TV station in Sioux Falls had a kid show in the afternoon called the Captain Eleven Show. They would bring in a bunch of kids and then the ones who had a birthday would get special attention. Carol and Loran took Lexi there on her birthday and she had just had tubes put in her ears because she was having trouble with them. The tubes just amplified every noise so when Captain Eleven saw her eyelashes He said,

"Those are the longest eyelashes I've ever seen," and started to pick her up. The kids all started to yell and scream and the noise was deafening to her and she clamped

her hands over her ears and began to cry. The Captain felt

really bad.

CHAPTER NINE

It was January of nineteen ninety one when Joel and Denise said their wedding vows. They chose Dallas to be the ring bearer, which seemed to be a good choice because he went through practice just fine. Then came the wedding day he and was all dressed up in his little tux and pillow in hand as he started down the aisle. He saw the people and he stopped and said. "I can't," and turned around and went back out into the foyer. He got so nervous he went into the bathroom and started vomiting. Chad Berhend was one of the ushers and he followed him and tried to console him and talk him into going down the aisle, but he just wouldn't be persuaded. Finally Chad pulled out a five dollar bill and said, "I'll give you this if you will go." Dallas looked at the bill and his eyes got big. He grabbed the bill, stuffed it in his pocket, set his jaw and almost ran down to the front.

It was May of that same year that Bryan and Diane were married. So that meant that eight of the kids were married. It is obvious that kids are far less conscious of skin color than adults. Janet's grandson was a classmate and playmate of Dallas' for several years. One day the grandson came home and announced, "Hey Mom, did you know that Dallas is adopted?"

Although Loran was going to a different church at this time, Carol was very diligent to see that the kids were active in her church. They went to Royal Rangers and Missionettes as well as being in church and Sunday school. Loran did come to all their special events, however, such as plays and programs.

Just as soon as he was old enough, mom had Dallas in soccer and he stayed with it until he was in high school. Dallas got pretty good at the game and was in high demand as a goalie.

As the kids became teenagers, a new youth pastor came to the church named Barry Holm. He turned out to be a tremendous influence in the kids' lives. It was at a youth camp that Barry was preaching when Kalee came to the altar and accepted the fact that God had a special calling on her life. Barry also became worship leader and his musical ability began to rub off on the kids. Joel began to play drums and Nathan soon followed. When Nate was getting ready to leave for college Loran took Barry aside and said, "why not give Dallas a chance to try out on the drums he seems to be getting the hang of it." Barry was very pleased with the result.

All too soon it came time for the girls to learn to drive. Loran took Kalee to the Perry Electric shop and turned her loose and let her drive around on the back lot. In no time at all she was good to go. Lexi took a little longer and her mom took her driving several times before she got the hang

of it. Mom had a few anxious moments when she was

learning what lane to drive in and such.

It was an ordinary Wednesday night and Kalee had driven

her little black Mercury to church even though it put her

driving after curfew on the way home. She was two blocks

from home when she got into a little fender bender at an

unmarked intersection. A college student hit her on the

side and pushed her up on the boulevard. She was so upset

to think that this could happen to her that she just left the

scene and ran home. She was hysterical by the time she got

home. Loran tried to comfort her but he knew she had to

go back to the accident to fill out the police report. As soon

as he got her settled down they walked back up the street.

The police had the tow truck there and wanted to tow the

car away but Loran talked them into letting him change the

tire and drive it home. This was a traumatic experience for

Kalee and was not soon forgotten.

The next traumatic event was when Lexi was again at an unmarked intersection with her little white Honda, and she t-boned an older gentleman in his little Ford. The worst of it was that she had Tonya's daughter, Whitney in the front seat with her. Whitney's nose hit the dashboard and she was bleeding and crying. Poor Lexi was beside herself. It took a while for Whitney to trust riding in the front seat again.

When Dallas learned to drive he started out with Kalee's black Mercury, but he became a victim when he was rear ended at a stop sign. After that Loran bought him a little blue Chevy pick up. One slippery morning he slid into a van at church. Another slippery evening he slid into a parked car by the Warehouse. The Warehouse was a youth center that the church operated in an old warehouse building owned by Perry Electric. Next Dallas became a victim again when he left his vehicle parked by the middle school and someone ran into it. Then Loran sold the little Chevy and bought a little GM pick up that looked just like it. This was one that Pam and Greg had owned and Greg had kept it in really good shape. When Dallas graduated from high school he bought a nice blue Chevy Blazer.

One day Lexi was driving down twenty second avenue which is four lane and a tractor came from the side and drove right up to the road looking like he wasn't going to stop so Lexi in an automatic reaction moved over in the other lane and side swiped an SUV. The family didn't get the best insurance rates for the next few years.

So there was a time when Nate and Tricia were in high school, Kalee and Lexi were in middle school, and Dallas in the primary grades and Carol had to car pool them plus the neighbor kids all to school. Seat belt laws weren't as strict then, so she would pile them all in the station wagon and head for school. A couple times she raised the eyebrows of a policeman watching as she unloaded them all at school.

The early nineties ushered the girls into teenage. It all seemed to happen so fast Loran and Carol were just busy working and paying the bills while the girls were developing into fine young women. Carol insisted that they take piano lessons even though neither one of them were very keen on the idea. But mom insisted so to lessons they went. Their piano teacher lived in Estelline, twenty four miles away so it became a major event to get them there especially when the weather was bad. Loran would drive them there and then wait in the car while they had their lessons. What they hated most were the recitals, but mom insisted, so they endured and came home with the trophies. Kalee started on saxaphome for a while and Lexi played trumpet in the high school marching band. She had a lot of cold early morning practices but she stuck with it for two full years.

In nineteen ninety five, Carol and Loran had been in separate churches for thirty three years but she and her prayer partners had never stopped praying for him. He was so sure that he was right that he couldn't see anything else. Then the church that he was so sure of began to change. Matter of fact it was as if God turned it upside down and shook it to get him out. So he began going to church with Carol at the Assembly of God church and never looked back at the thirty three wasted years.

In nineteen ninety seven, Carol was teaching kids church and she had the kids sitting on the floor in a circle. She accidently tripped over one of the kids and injured her foot. Although they put a walking cast on it, it never healed right and she began to have trouble with it. By two thousand three she had five surgeries on it, putting pins in it, taking

pins out, and finally a plate. In the struggle to get her foot

fixed her back started giving her trouble and in two

thousand two she had back surgery that put her in a wheel

chair that she has never really graduated from. In two

thousand three she spent four weeks at the Avera

McKennon pain clinic learning to cope with chronic pain

but it never really changed anything that much.

Barry Holm was still the youth pastor at the church during

this time and he had a real active group going. Lexi not

only helped with the youth group a lot but she babysat his

children almost constantly so his wife Alyssa could help

minister.

Nineteen ninety nine found Kalee graduating from high

school, Lexi was just a year behind, and Dallas was a

teenager and began working at Perry Electric after school.

So the class of two thousand of Brookings High School

included Lexi Perry.

Kalee went on to enroll at South Dakota State University while Lexi enrolled in a discipleship program at the Assembly of God church in Sioux Falls called Masters Commission. Loran and Carol cried when they drove away and left her at her host home. She had grown up so fast. The next year was worse when she started her nurses' training at North Central University in Minneapolis. Carol wasn't able to travel so they had to send Nathan to take her to the school. She ended up staying right in the scary part of downtown, and had a job in restaurant in the Mall Of America. She rode the bus back and forth late at night. God was faithful, however, and kept her safe. During these two years she took mission trips to England, Spain, Jerusalem, and the Dominican Republic. She then came back to Sioux Falls to continue her nurse training at Southeast Technical Institute, and graduated the following year from Dakota State in Mitchell. Upon graduation she went to work at Avera Mckennon Hospital. After a year at Mckennon she went to Sanford Hospital to work in the new children's unit.

Meanwhile Kalee graduated from SDSU and was working at First National Bank in Brookings. While she was in high school she had gone on a mission trip to Mexico with the youth group and it changed her life. She had a good friend whose parents adopted two children from Haiti and Kalee had many chances to baby sit them and interact with them. She began to get a passion for the children of Haiti. She moved to Sioux Falls and got a job at an insurance company and her first trip to Haiti was with a group from Wisconsin. While she was there she helped in an orphanage and her love the Haitian children intensified. She went back to Haiti a second time, again helping in an orphanage and caring for the Haitian children.

While all this was going on, Nate who had been working at Perry Electric decided to go to Bible school and he chose Christ for the Nations Institute in Dallas Texas. He graduated with a two year degree, and in two thousand Three he married Stephanie Rosello, who also completed a two year degree at CF & I. They are still living in Dallas and have two children and Nate works for an insurance company in building maintenance, putting his electrical skills to work that he learned from Dad. Meanwhile Dallas decided he would like to go to Bible school also so he completed a two year degree at CF&I also and is living in Dallas and working at the Airport.

After twelve years of ministry in Texas and Michigan, Tricia returned to Sioux Falls, Married Steve Henning, a school teacher, went through nursing school and is working at Sanford Hospital also. Joel, after working at Perry Electric for a few years, is a policeman for the city of

Brookings, He and his wife Denise have two children. Pam

has two children and she and her husband Greg own a

series of gyms in Brookings and surrounding area. Tonya

has two children and after working at Perry Electric for

several years now works with Pam in her gyms. Bryan,

after working at Perry Electric for many years, works for

the Federal Government at Northern Grain Insect

Laboratory in Brookings. He and his wife Diane have two

adopted Chinese children. I wonder where they got the

adoption idea. Laurie lives in St Paul Minnesota where her

husband Dave Schaefer is an executive at 3M. They have

three children. Keven and his wife Deb own and operate

Perry Electric and have three children. Doug lives in

Livermore California with his wife Yolanda and works in

computer software development. Doug has one son.

June 2001 was a pinnacle moment for Loran. His children

nominated him, and he was commissioned "Dad of the

year," for father's day 2001 by the local newspaper. He was featured on the front page with a huge family photo including all the spouses and grand kids. It was an awesome experience and welcome reward for the years of toil and the care and concern he had put into raising his family. It really made the devil angry though, because a lot of bad things happened to him right after that.

So, once again Carol and Loran have to look back at where God has taken them on this life saving, family raising mission. They can see now very plainly God's calling, His provision, His protection, and His ultimate blessing. They are equally proud of each one of their children. They gave them their start in life and the children, to the best of their abilities individually and collectively have "taken the ball and run with it." Again you can see that there is no difference between their biological and their adopted children. They were all treated equally and were able to excel individually to their own abilities. When Carol and Loran look back at where the adopted kids would be had they not persevered in getting them home they can rest assured that it was all worth it. The biggest blessing of Carol and Loran's whole life was when they read Matthew 25:35-40 and obeyed it. "For I was hungry and you gave me food, I was thirsty and you gave me drink, I was a stranger and you took me in, I was naked and you clothed me, I was sick and you visited me, I was in prison and you came to me. Then Carol and Loran will answer Him saying, 'Lord when did we see you hungry and feed you, or thirsty and give you drink? When did we see you a stranger and take you in?, or naked and clothe you? Or when did we see you sick or in prison and come to you?' And the King will answer and say to them, 'assuredly, I say to you Carol and Loran, inasmuch as you have done it unto the least of these my brethren, you have done it onto me."

May the Lord bless your life as you do as Carol and Loran have done, simply take commands from His word and obey them.

Made in the USA
Charleston, SC
11 March 2010